Printed in the USA

ISBN 978-1-7934965-5-3

Graphic Design by Lucas Taccardi

Cover art/illustrationsby Phil Anderson Blythe
THEOHUXXX ART

Author Photograph by Rob Himebaugh

TABLE OF CONTENTS

THE CHANGING OF THE SEASONS

a collection.

the light, it fades.

PINOT

It doesn't take much

To get me laughing

A bottle of wine

A bowl of weed

Are all I need

To make me happy

Glistening red velvet

Spilling out of the glass

My body warms

With a single pass

Expand my mind

Open my heart

Lovers at last

'Till death do we part

SAIL THE SKY

Lying in the grass

Basking in afternoon sun

Thoughts of what I miss

I have only one

You by my side

Drawing pictures in the sky

Will you be mine?

My partner in crime

Together, we conquer the world

New memories and the like

Just me and my girl

Lets fly away

High within the clouds

Away from all the mess

Away from all the crowds

Our bodies entwined together

Here we can live forever

LUST

_____

This is the moment

I have been waiting for

When our bodies melt

And our hearts fill with fire

With actions fueled by pure lust

I look through your eyes

And into your soul

With each passing thrust

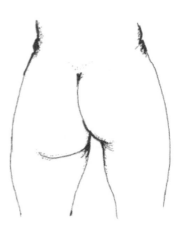

THE LITTLE THINGS

Dollar Slices

Between bars

Is like her

Sucking you off

Between positions

BLISS

Such sweet

Moments of bliss

Feigning ignorance

To all of this

Our lives interwoven

Are not meant to last

These feelings and our love

Will too, soon pass

TEMPORARY LOVER

Another door closes

Meanwhile,

Your legs are spread open

Part of your rotation

Lost within the crowd

From one to another and on to the next

You'll see me again

By then I will be just like the others

Another face of a temporary lover

AND YET,

———————

I remain lost in her stare

I melt in her arms

Her call leaves me breathless

Her touch leaves me senseless

A dog at her feet

A slave to her needs

I lay with filthy beasts

Upon the shit and piss

I should be smarter

But I deserve this

REGRET

Wasted time

Wasted memories

Wasted kisses

Wasted everything

MR. MISERY

Another piece of me

Has died

Another woman

Walked out of my life

Cold heart

Warm eyes

A sordid soul

In disguise

You took my love and stole my heart

You ripped and tore it all apart

Now I sit

And ponder what is done

Just me, myself, and I

A pity party for one

Alone, alone

Better off on my own

Love is not for me

My name is Mr. Misery

THE TRUTH

———————

I am afraid

To get close

Because I know

The moment I do

They will see me

For who I really am

Turning their backs

In disgust

Deepening this shade of blue

WORMS

Here we are at the end

Is it what we expected?

Did life turn out

The way we planned it?

Are we who we should be?

People of Honor?

People of dignity?

Or are we just

Swill, filth, Scum, waste

Worms in the dirt

All these things I hate

BLAZE

———————

All I want is

Acceptance

All I get are

Denies

Sometimes I wish

I could kill you

Sometimes I wish

I could cry

So high

I feel like lifting

So low

The mood is shifting

My toes graze the water

Preparing for the splash

Or maybe I'll set myself aflame

And blaze into ash

RUNAWAY

———————

Up, down, all around

Run away

Somewhere I can't be found

The sky

The earth

The water

The ground

To live in darkness

And never make a sound

PEARLY WHITE

———————

But don't forget to smile first

One laugh for the world to see

Grin those pearly white shit-eaters

Make them happy, pretend to care

Anything to prove you're really there

ANGELS WITH FILTHY SOULS

I am a good boy

Mama told me so

What should I have done?

How was I to know?

Following sensation and desire

Would bring me to the place

Where hearts and souls retire?

The machine grinds

The flesh of those who've fallen

Here I am,

On my knees, I'll come crawling

Begging forgiveness

To regain a sense of joy

Mama Please!

I swear I'll be a good boy

THE CHANGING OF THE SEASONS

———

Celebration

Contemplation

Constipation

Meditation

Masturbation

Expiration

WHITE PLEATHER

White Pleather

Porno Staple

Disguises cum and spit

Highlights dirt and shit

Under fluorescent light

Skin and fabric

Melt together

Dripping sweat upon

White Pleather

SKEET

Two Earth-first

Tree-hugging

Teeny-bopping

Hippies

Plot to stop

The big bad

Tree-chopping

Woodsman

Offering their bodies and

Submitting their holes in

Sexual sacrifice

Saving the earth

One fuck at a time

OLD DOGS

Two old dogs and a Porn Star

Go for a walk

Meanwhile,

The girls are just leaving school

One would think this was planned

OCCUPATIONAL HAZARD

Fucked my girl

And it was fun

So much fun

I wanted to cum

So cum I did

But mistake I made

There was no camera to film

No pictures to take

My top burst and ropes shot to the sky

"Jesus, what the hell is wrong with this

guy?"

I worked, I pulled

She sucked, she blew

But my fleshy little friend was through

Great,

Now what are we supposed to do?

IT'S AS SIMPLE AS

Suck

Fuck

Swallow

Smile

EXPECTATIONS

What I crave is

Admire, Admire, Admire

What I create is

Defile, Defile, Defile

No love, no love

Just

Porn, Porn, Porn

Dick in my hand

I need

More, More, More

HOLE

———————

I desire a hole

In which to dump my seed

I want you to beg

Your hungry mouth to feed

Eyes tearing

Makeup smeared

I want to watch you plead

Stick out your tongue

So I may spit

Rest your feet upon my thighs

As you sit

On your knees

Press your face to the floor

This shower of pearls

Is all for you, whore

Lick the tile clean

Make them sparkle with your tongue

Recollect, orgasm over

I'm done

EAT ME ALIVE

———

In the morning,

I discover little white lies

Scattered about my groin and taint

Preventing me from working

Withholding my pay

My body

Has aligned against me

Has sent me signals for years

What I am doing

Will eat me alive

Will bring me to tears

BOY-TOY

———————

Happy, Happy, Joy, Joy

It's good to be a boy-toy

Gun in my hand

Aimed at your face

On your knees

Time to get a taste

Savor it

Don't spill a drop

Poison with my seed

This disease will never stop

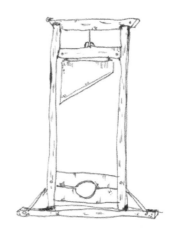

the darkness, it grows.

EVENING WINE

Evening wine

Celebration for the swine

Drinking, shooting, guzzling booze

Inevitably, he will lose

Out of sight, out of mind

The only thing he's truly out of

Is time

Living in the dark

He can't see the light

Bills to pay, no money to earn

A poor man's plight

NEWBORN

In the morning,

Nose is dry, bloody, and cracked

Head throbs, body sore

We drank the ocean,

Snorted the sky,

Smoked the Earth, and more

A vacation, an escape

In other words, a rebirth

So, it is only fitting we should wake

Crying like the newborn

THE WARMTH

I wake

With no motivation

To work or play

Only wish to rest in the warmth all day

Oversized Flannels

Hide my lack of definition

Cloaking my absence of discipline

Finding solace in an upturned bottle

Letting the drink guide my way

THE PLIGHT

———————

Everybody

Wants to rule

The world

But nobody

Wants to leave

Their couch

TELEVISION

My brain melts with

Each passing three-minute pitch

Hypnotism for couch potatoes

And here I thought

Porn was desensitizing

THE WANDERER

I am but a man

Alone, without a path

Lost within this sea of lights

I can never go back

They call me the wanderer

Nothing but a ponderer

Musings of a hard life and

Love lost

Seeking answers and

Satisfaction

At the ultimate cost

I am a mere superstition

A walking breathing contradiction

THE FENCE

———————

I know change must begin with me

I know change will set me free

I know this and yet I'm on the fence

I prefer the safety of indifference

FIXED

———————

Erase the past

Become someone else

Create, transform

Lose yourself

But nothing and no one

Can set me free

I am what I am

And that's all I'll ever be

STASIS

———

Black spaces

Warped faces

Dirty places

Paper chases

Free bases

Mind erases

HOPE (LESS)

I intoxicate to eradicate

I masturbate to alleviate

No money, no hope

Just a dirty dick

And a bag full of dope

I should pour my heart

Instead I tug my cock

Seeking catharsis of the mind

I settle for procrasturbation of time

PAPER CHASE

I should be chasing paper

To shrink my growing debt

Instead I am complacent

Squandering what is left

I dig myself deeper

As signs of light disappear

Please leave me alone

So I may rot here

With each passing day

My human qualities subside

I am slowly becoming

Becoming the monster I despise

TIME

Time melts

With no indication of slowing

I shuffle through life

Unsure of where I am going

What will I do

When I am through?

Oh, that's easy

I'll waste time

Jerking off

To thoughts of you

THE CITY

Los Angeles is

Nothing more than

Solo-motorists and

Self-Medicators

I think the city

Has ruined me

Earlier,

I had a runny nose

So,

I took half a Viagra

Now,

I have a splitting headache

A raging hard-on

And I want to kill myself

IRONY

Civilian wants to fuck

Bar full of potential

She settles on one

A Bona-fide legend

A Boner-iffic stud

Peddler of the flesh

Expectations are high

But the reality is

He can't keep it up

His wood falls

His eyes tire

Just an aging meat puppet

Set to expire

THE WORDS

The words pass through me

And the moment I realize their weight

They've already left, out of reach

Wish I could grab them by their tails

And pull them back

But they are gone, fleeting

While I remain bleeding

I spit, rhyme, cuss

And make a fuss

But when I sit

To channel and record

Inspiration flees

Never more, never more

I wish I could say

What is on my mind

Instead of searching for words

Wasting time

Desperate for what

I will never find

PRETTY

I sit in my corner

And wallow in self-pity

But at least my reflection

In the mirror

Still looks pretty

THE MACHINE

———————

Try so hard to clean myself

To rid my body of these stains

Words of my failures

Written upon my flesh

A daily reminder for me

My black heart for all to see

I finally break the surface

Tear a hole, peel it open

Peer at what's inside

Nothing

But the broken down

Innards

Of a filthy, rust infected

Machine

THE STRANGER

I am a stranger in my own skin

Unfamiliar with what dwells within

I am haunted, manic, evil to the core

Cold to the touch

I am your Dollar Store Whore

AXE

What once gave a name, an identity

Is now the same axe swung for death

What once brought life

Now brings hate, pain,

An eternity of shame

MARROW

Darkness returns

Breaking my bones

Sucking my marrow

Swallowing me whole

RUN

My mind

A jumbled mess

Can't think straight

Only stress

Past mistakes and

Failures to come

I'll do what I do best

Run, Run, Run

RALPH

Guilty Conscience

Losing track of time

Can't sleep at night

Too much on the mind

Killed the mother

With your bare hands

Your unborn child

And you call yourself a man?

Users, Abusers

Tattoos with no name

Is any of it special?

Or must it all end the same?

What about her?

What about her eyes?

When she looked at you

Said she loved you

Did you think they were lies?

I hope you're happy

You sick, rabid dog

Little puppy has gotten himself lost

Deep within the shrouding fog

The clock is winding down

Now what will you do?

I hope you're watching

Soon you'll get what's coming to you

PERPLEXITY

Tugging

In front of the mirror

Watching myself drain

Until there is nothing

But a hollow shell

Please help me

I am in hell

With all these mirrors

I think I have friends

With all these mirrors

At least I can pretend

White walls and blank spaces

Dirty knees and warped faces

Dreams and bigger aspirations

All I have left now

Is masturbation

Such perplexity, what a bind

Jerk myself until I am blind

Liberation!

I can no longer see

No mirrors, nor reflections

I am finally free

WAVES

—————

Waves,

Crash at my feet

Claw, pull

Carry me away

Wash my sin

My leaching sores

Take me, break me

Feed me, fuck me

Make me yours

MY WORST ENEMY

My dreams, they haunt me

No imagination to be free

Confined in my thoughts

Trapped with my worst enemy

Disappearing at a rapid pace

God, I cannot wait to leave this place

No one will miss me when I am gone

This is my sad sad song

PEST

———————

I am the filth

You try to wash away

The pest

You wish to eradicate

I am a walking reminder

Of all the things we hate

All the dark and seedy thoughts

Kept suppressed below the waist

My mind crumbles in stages

But I still have time to fill these pages

My words, my sweat

My blood, my cum

Soon all of this will be done

about the author

J.R. Verlin is a writer living in Los Angeles, and for the better part of a decade, he has been gracing box covers and front pages of X-rated Tube sites across the world as his lascivious alter ego, Logan Pierce.

Further reading at Whoislogan.com